My Pet Rat

My Pet Rat

by **Arlene Erlbach**

photographs by **Andy King**

All About Pets

Lerner Publications Company • Minneapolis

To Debbie Ducommun, the Rat Lady, for all her helpful and ratful information

Acknowledgments

Special thanks to the Spiro family, the O'Connor family, Erica Bush and Alphonsia, Megan O'Connor, Becky Cozen, and Herb Erlbach, for finding the Rat Site. Thanks also to the Humane Society of the United States; the Wilmette Pet Shop, Wilmette, Illinois; the Barking Lot; Ginger Cardinal and the American Rat, Mouse & Hamster Society; Mary Ann Isaksen and the Fancy Rat and Mouse Association; and the Rat Fan Club. The publisher would like to thank Rachel Shellum and Doug Shellum, who were photographed for this book; Pet Outfitters, Burnsville, Minnesota; Beth Westlund; and Dr. Barb Leppke.

Photos on pages 8 (right), 10 (left), 11(left), 18, and 21 (left) by Jerry Boucher; p. 12 (left), 15, 22 (left), 26 (left), 37 (both), 40 (all), 46 (both), and 58 by Jim Simondet, Independent Picture Service; p. 20 (left) by Michael Gilroy, reproduced with permission of Aquila Photographics; p. 20 (top and lower right) © Joan Balzarini.

website address: www.lernerbooks.com

Library of Congress Cataloging-in-Publication Data

Erlbach, Arlene.
    My pet rat / by Arlene Erlbach ; photographs by Andy King.
      p.   cm. — (All about pets)
    Summary: Text and photographs follow a twelve-year-old girl as she learns to care for her pet rat.
      Includes bibliographical references (p.   ) and index.
      ISBN 0–8225–2260–8 (alk. paper)
      1. Rats as pets—Juvenile literature. [1. Rats as pets.
    2. Pets.] I. King, Andy, ill. II. Title. III. Series.
SF459.R3E75 1998
636.9'352—dc21   97–24709

Manufactured in the United States of America
1 2 3 4 5 6 — JR — 03 02 01 00 99 98

Contents

Kirby is a fancy rat...

My name is Rachel and I'm 12 years old. I love animals. I have a cat named Bianca who lives with me at my mom's house. I have two hamsters named Herbie and Knobby. They're named after Kent Hrbek and Chuck Knoblauch, two of my favorite baseball players. I live with my hamsters at my dad's house, on the weekends and during school vacations. My parents are divorced.

Our arrangement works pretty well for my pets. If they all lived together, Bianca would probably try to hurt Herbie and Knobby. My mom doesn't like hamsters anyway. But my dad doesn't mind them, so his place is the best for them. He even suggested buying a rat.

This is my rat, Kirby.

An aquarium is the perfect rat cage. I've seen rats in cages with bars, and the rats chew on the bars and bend them.

"Rats are very playful and intelligent," Dad said. He's a psychologist, and he remembers doing experiments with rats when he was in college.

My friend Erica has a rat. Erica's rat, Alphonsia, is cute and fun to play with, so I was sure I'd like having a rat, too.

For Christmas, my dad gave me a 15-gallon aquarium with a mesh screen on top. It had a gift certificate inside, from Pet Outfitters, for one rat. But the gift certificate was dated for March! My dad said rats need lots of attention, especially at first. It would be best to buy our rat during my spring break. Since I would be at my dad's the whole week, I would have more time to be with our new rat then.

Until March, I spent time learning about rats. My dad and I read books on them. I asked Erica all about her rat, and we played with Alphonsia a lot. I decided to buy just one rat at first, like Erica did. If you buy two or more rats, they have to be the same sex, or you have to get them neutered or spayed. Otherwise, they'll mate. You'll end up with *a lot* more rats than you want. Rats enjoy the company of other rats, but they seem happy with just humans to play with.

My dad learned about rats with me. He would take care of my rat when I stayed at my mom's.

On the Saturday that started my spring break, my dad took me to Pet Outfitters to buy my rat. The store kept the baby rats in a big aquarium. They were about six weeks old, and they were all different colors. I was a little surprised, because I expected them all to be white like Alphonsia. But the pet store had white rats, gray rats, tan rats, and rats with spots.

I watched the rats for a few minutes. Some of the rats played with each other, and others were asleep. I liked a chubby brown and white one that seemed to be watching the other rats.

The rats at the store were about two months old. I watched them a while to pick out my favorite.

The baby rats were all so cute! But I liked the very first one I held.

The pet shop clerk lifted that rat out of the aquarium for me. He showed me how to cup the rat in two hands so it would feel safe and wouldn't jump out of my hands.

"It's so tiny," I told the clerk.

"She only weighs 2 ounces," the clerk said.

The clerk told me that this rat was a female hooded rat. It didn't matter to me if I got a boy or a girl. The books I'd read said that female and male rats are equally intelligent and they both make good pets. I liked this rat. I decided right away to name her Kirby, after Kirby Puckett, who played baseball for the Minnesota Twins.

I knew what supplies to buy, since I'd read about setting up a rat cage. Ground corn cobs are good for rats.

At the pet store, we bought all the things I needed for Kirby: rat food pellets, food dishes, a water bottle with a tube, aspen chips to line the bottom of her aquarium, and some hay.

I'd read somewhere that it's best not to use pine or cedar chips to line a rat's aquarium. They contain oils that can cause respiratory problems—infections or diseases that affect breathing. Respiratory problems can shorten your rat's life. Aspen chips are better for rats, and so are ground corn cobs and alfalfa pellets. I've heard corn cobs and alfalfa pellets will turn a rat's tail and feet green! This doesn't hurt the rat, though.

The hay we bought is for Kirby to curl up in. Rats like to make nests from hay, or from something else that's like hay. Some people use ink-free paper strips instead of hay for their rats. Erica tears the ends from computer paper to give to Alphonsia. Shredded paper towels are also nice for a rat to curl up and tunnel in.

Your rat doesn't have to have hay. But it doesn't cost much, and rats like it for nesting.

Aquariums come in lots of sizes. A rat needs a tank at least 10 gallons big.

Rats are inexpensive compared to many pets. They don't cost a lot themselves—just a few dollars. All together, the equipment and supplies we bought cost around $20. This was not including the aquarium, of course. That cost about $20 by itself. But some of the things—like the aquarium, food dishes, and water bottle—I wouldn't need to buy again. I could use them at least two to three years, which is about how long pet rats live. The food, aspen chips, and hay for Kirby would only cost $6 to $7 each month.

Choosing the Right Rat

Rats come in more than 20 color variations. They range from all-white or hooded (with dark hair on the head and back, and white lower bodies) to having many other colors. Some rats have coloring like Siamese cats. Other rats have dalmation spots.

It's easy to be attracted to a rat because of its coloring. But when you choose a rat, look for health and personality.

- Watch the rats carefully. Watch to see which ones are drinking from their water bottle and eating rat pellets. If you don't see a rat eat or drink, it may not be weaned (eating and drinking foods besides its mother's milk), and it will die from starvation.

- A healthy rat doesn't sneeze, wheeze, have diarrhea, or have runny eyes or a runny nose. These are all signs that your rat is sick. If your pet rat shows signs of illness, you need to call a veterinarian.

- A healthy rat will have a sleek, glossy coat and be curious and active. Choose a rat that seems friendly toward you—not one that backs off.

- A baby rat might nibble on your fingers. That's okay. But don't choose a rat that bites. If a rat licks you, this means it's kissing. That might be the rat for you.

- Domesticated rats usually live for about two to three years. Some have lived longer. Before you buy a rat, ask yourself if you'll be interested in it for its entire life span.

Rats in the wild usually have shorter lifespans than pet rats, because wild rats may be eaten by other animals such as snakes or hawks. Actually, a good place to buy a rat is a pet shop that sells snakes and rats as snake food. You'd be saving a rat that would otherwise end up as a snake's lunch!

I bought two clay bowls, not plastic ones, for Kirby's food. The clerk at the store told me that rats love to chew on things, and a rat could easily destroy a plastic bowl. A clay bowl is also heavy enough that the rat can't tip it over.

Dad let me buy treats for Kirby, since it was a special day.

We didn't buy the toys I wanted. But we had all the things our rat needed.

The pet store clerk put Kirby in a cardboard box with a handle on it. He said, "You're buying a fancy rat."

"Fancy" doesn't have to do with Kirby being a particular breed or color. A fancy rat is a pet rat. *Fancied* means "liked." So people who have pet rats are rat fanciers.

On the way home in the car, I told Kirby about all the fun we would have together. I told her about the aquarium that I was going to get ready for her. I told Kirby that she was a fancy rat, but I don't think she cared.

Rats like a separate bedroom...

Rats will tunnel and burrow, even inside a cage.

A rat's aquarium isn't just a place for it to sleep. It's the rat's whole house. So I needed to make separate sleeping and eating areas when I set up Kirby's aquarium. Many rats in the wild live in underground homes called burrows. They dig separate rooms in the dirt for sleeping and eating. They even have a bathroom. Then they dig tunnels to connect their rooms.

I decided to keep Kirby's aquarium on my dresser. There, it would be away from the window and near my bed. Rats, like hamsters, shouldn't be near drafts, or they can get respiratory sicknesses. Rats don't like bright light, either, and they are very sensitive to heat and humidity. Temperatures over 90 degrees can kill a rat.

The best temperature for a rat is between 65 and 80 degrees. That's the temperature we keep our house anyway—around 70 degrees. Rats are like people this way—they're comfortable when we're comfortable. So you wouldn't want to keep a rat in your basement. The rat would get too cold.

My room is the best place to keep my rat.

Rat Facts

- Female rats usually weigh from ½ to ¾ pound.
- Males usually weigh from 1 to 1½ pounds. But some male rats have grown as big as 2 pounds.
- Rats stop growing at about 8 months.
- Baby rats are called pups.
- A group of rats born together is called a litter.

- Rats use their tail for balance. A rat's tail is so strong that it's almost like an extra arm. But never pick up your rat by its tail. That can really hurt your rat.
- Rats are a lot like people. In the wild, they live in family groups. Older brothers or sisters watch out for the safety of siblings. Sometimes the father rat snuggles with the babies to keep them warm.

- A female rat can start having babies at about 3 months.
- Look at your rat's tail closely. It has short hairs. These hairs help your rat find its way in the dark.

I spread a layer of aspen chips over the bottom of Kirby's aquarium. I made it about ½ inch thick. People call this layer of chips "bedding." I call it Kirby's carpet, because it covers the floor of her house. I know that Kirby will find an area of the carpet herself to go to the bathroom in. That's what the chips are for, mostly. They absorb odors.

Rats also like a separate place for a bed, like an old milk carton or an oatmeal box. They like an old rag or sock stuffed inside with them. This makes a rat feel safe and comfy. Sometimes rats like to hide in their beds. I gave Kirby an old knit hat for her bed. That's what Erica does for Alphonsia.

It's easy to set up a rat's cage. The chips make a rat feel at home.

A water bottle will keep your rat's cage neat. Rats aren't the best housekeepers, but they like clean food and water.

I added a few handfuls of hay to Kirby's aquarium. Then I placed a clay food bowl in one corner of the cage and attached Kirby's water bottle to the side. Rats and hamsters shouldn't be fed water from a dish, I've learned. They love to drop things into water, like food and bedding. The water bowl gets to be a mess! My hamsters did that at first, until I got them a bottle.

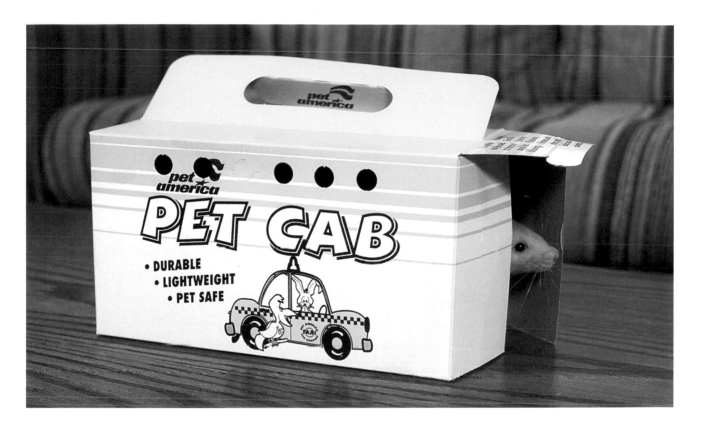

Kirby seemed afraid to come out at first.

The whole time I was setting up the aquarium that first day, I told Kirby what I was doing. She was still inside the box from the pet store. But she was watching me through the holes. I kept the door to my room closed, just in case she escaped from her box. Kirby wasn't used to me or my room yet. If she got loose, she'd probably try to hide or make a getaway.

Once the cage was ready, I opened the box and picked Kirby up gently. I cupped her in my hands so she would feel safe. Then I gently set her down in the aquarium and I gave her food and water.

Kirby was curious about her new cage. Then she groomed herself.

For the first few minutes, she explored the aquarium and nibbled at some food. Then she groomed herself by licking her body, toes, and tail. Rats groom themselves many times a day. Their teeth and paws are their comb. They lick, nibble, pull, and scratch their fur.

Kirby needed some time to herself to explore her new house. That's what all my rat books told me. So I left her alone for a while, and I didn't take her out to play that night. The next day, Kirby and I could start getting to know each other. We had a whole week for that.

I worked on our friendship...

When I woke up the next morning, Kirby was still asleep. She was all curled up in her bed, the hat. I wanted to wake her up so I could play with her. But I didn't want to scare or startle her.

After a few minutes, while I was getting dressed, Kirby started to wake up by herself. She walked around the aquarium. Like any rat, she's very curious.

"Good morning," I said.

I put my hand into the aquarium. Kirby wasn't familiar with me yet. So she ran back into the hat.

Kirby hid in her hat a lot, especially at first.

I decided that Kirby was going to need coaxing, with food, to be my friend. So I went into the kitchen and got a handful of wheat flakes. My dad told me rats like all kinds of cereals that aren't too sugary. Erica says Alphonsia likes wheat flakes best. I held just one wheat flake in Kirby's cage. She took it from my fingers and nibbled it.

Kirby likes the same cereals
I do: corn or wheat flakes,
puffs, Chex, or Cheerios.

Kirby would have to get used to my scent. Rats have keen noses, and they recognize each other by smell.

While Kirby was eating, I told her how pretty I think she is, and how much she must be enjoying her wheat flake. My dad came into the room then. He gave Kirby another wheat flake and we both watched her nibble.

I was hoping that Kirby would let me pet her then. I put my hand into the aquarium very gently and slowly. Jerky movements scare rats. Kirby scampered to the corner of her aquarium. At least she didn't go into the hat or hay to hide. But I could see she didn't trust me yet.

After about half an hour of watching and talking to Kirby, my dad and I left her alone. It's best to let a rat get to know you gradually. If I came on too strong, Kirby could have nipped my hand. That happened with my hamster Knobby when I first got him, and it hurt. Hamsters and rats are both rodents, so they are kind of similar. Rats are much more friendly with people, though.

That evening, I gave Kirby more wheat flake treats before I filled her food bowl. She seemed curious about me. She sniffed my hand a little. But when I tried to pick her up, she scurried back into the hat.

If a rat is scared or angry, it will bite.

I try to wear old clothes when I play with Kirby, since rats will chew on fabric.

The next morning, I woke up early. I offered Kirby a piece of cooked spaghetti. I had called Erica the night before, and she told me that rats like food that wiggles. Kirby sniffed my hand longer than before, so I thought I could pick her up. I put one hand over her back. Then I slid my other hand gently under her front legs and lifted her up. I held her against my shoulder and petted her head with my finger. After a minute, she tried to get away. I was a little upset about that. But Kirby and I were closer to becoming friends.

Three times a day for three days, I worked on our friendship. I picked her up and held her and petted her. Most of the time, Kirby let me hold her longer and longer.

By the fourth day, Kirby wasn't afraid of me and eagerly climbed onto my hand. Even though we were getting pretty friendly, I didn't put her up to my face. I still thought she might try to bite or scratch me.

Now that Kirby is comfortable with me, she'll play with me any time. Kirby likes it when I scratch behind her ears and under her chin. She lets me know by grinding her teeth together. They make a clicking sound. This is Kirby's way of talking to me and saying, "I like you. I'm having fun." Sometimes Kirby nuzzles and licks my hand.

Once a rat gets to know you, it likes to be held.

Rat Shows

Rats are becoming popular pets, because they don't require a great deal of care and are inexpensive, intelligent, and affectionate. According to pet shop owners and breeders of rats, mice, hamsters, and Guinea pigs, rats are the most affectionate rodent pet. Rats have become so popular, some people have started clubs and rat newsletters. Kids are welcome to join these organizations and subscribe to the newsletters. You do not need to live in the club's area to join.

Some of the rat clubs organize rat shows, which are similar to dog and cat shows. They set official standards for judging, such as what sizes and types of coloring they're looking for.

If there are no rat shows in your area, you may be able to organize one at a local pet store. Your show doesn't need to have official standards. You can still give prizes for the biggest, most unusual, or friendliest rat. Some participants can even show off their rats' tricks. Give certificates and take pictures of all the rats so everyone will have a special souvenir of the event.

EST GROOMING
"Buddy"

MOST INTELLIGENT
"Mickey"

BIGGEST TEETH
"Bernice"

I got my dad to start playing with Kirby, too, after he came home from work. When I went back to school and to my mom's house, my dad would take care of Kirby for me—except when I came back on weekends. So Kirby needed to know my dad well.

My dad and Kirby got along from the start.

Homework is better with a rat on your shoulder. But sometimes the rat won't stay there.

A few weekends later, I decided to train Kirby to ride on my shoulder. I made sure I wore a long-sleeved top when I did this, because Kirby's claws are sharp.

I put her on my shoulder, but she wouldn't stay there at first. She climbed up and down like we were playing a game. Finally she balanced on my shoulder. So I took her for a ride around my room. Rats must have a good sense of balance, because she didn't fall.

After about a month, Kirby was very comfortable with me. She would crawl up and down my arm and snuggle up to my neck. I could even put her on my shoulder while I read or watched television. She still tries to do this a lot. Sometimes she crawls inside my shirt. That tickles, but it's fun.

I call the mixture rat stew...

Loose grains and pellets shouldn't be a rat's only food.

Kirby eats anything. All rats will. But you can't give a rat just anything to eat, because it could get sick. Rats need about a quarter cup of small rat pellets each day. They also need a little bit of people food.

I buy Kirby's rat food from a bin of pellets at the pet store. It's best to buy pellets made especially for rats. Pellets made for hamsters, mice, and gerbils don't have all the right nutrients for rats. But rat pellets come close. I buy some rodent mix, too. These are little biscuits made from different kinds of grains and seeds.

I've heard it's best not to give loose, prepared-grain mixtures to rats as their only food. Some rats have favorite seeds. If they can separate them, they'll just eat their favorites and leave the rest. They won't get a balanced diet that way.

I buy one pound of rat food at a time, which is enough to last about a month. I also buy about a quarter pound of grain mixture. If you buy too much food at once, it will get stale. If a rat eats stale food and gets sick, it won't touch that kind of food again. So I need to make sure that Kirby's food is always fresh. I store the food I buy in a canister with a tight lid.

Pet Outfitters sells lots of rat food, so I can be pretty sure their food is fresh.

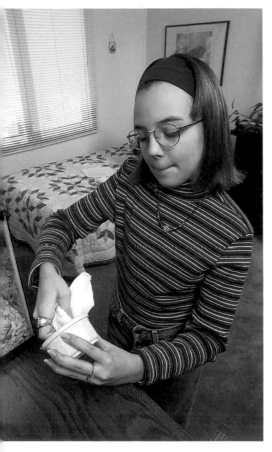

The biggest thing to remember about pets is they depend on you for everything. Rats need fresh food and water every night.

Every night, either my dad or I wipe out Kirby's dish with a clean damp rag. Then we add her new food. We change the water in her bottle and wipe off the tube. Every time I do this, Kirby is very glad to see me. She knows it's dinnertime, and time for attention.

Kirby doesn't gobble all her food at once. But by morning it will be gone. Rats are nibblers. They eat little by little. Kirby eats a little food when I fill her bowl, then she saves the rest for later. Rats are nocturnal animals, which means they're active mostly at night. They like to eat at night, too.

Rat Chow

Here's a homemade diet that's terrific for rats. If you use it, you won't need to buy pellets or grain mixture.

Every day, feed your rat:
- ⅛ slice whole wheat bread
- 5-8 flakes multi-grain cereal
- 1 teaspoon fruit
- 3 teaspoons vegetables
- One tablespoon homemade rat mix (recipe below)

4-5 times a week*, feed your rat:
- 1 canned oyster
- or 1 small piece cooked liver

*2 times a week for rats 6 months or older.

Recipe for One Week of Homemade Rat Mix

What you'll need:
- 5 teaspoons uncooked oatmeal
- ½ teaspoon sunflower seeds
- 3 teaspoons crushed barley
- 2 teaspoons millet
- 5 teaspoons cooked brown rice
- 2 tablespoons toasted wheat germ
- 3½ teaspoons brewer's yeast
- 700 mg calcium from chewable tablets
- 1 tablespoon dark molasses

What you'll do:
Grind up calcium tablets in a blender. Mix in rice and dry ingredients. Add molasses and mix thoroughly. Store in a covered container in the refrigerator.

Kirby needs fresh fruits and vegetables in addition to rat food. Every other day we give her a few teaspoons of fruits and vegetables—a strawberry, a slice of banana, or a slice of apple or tomato. She'll eat them separately or mixed. We usually cut pieces of Kirby's favorite fruits and vegetables and mix them up. I call the mixture rat stew. We put a few spoonfuls of Kirby's rat stew in another bowl beside her pellet dish.

Kirby eats anything I give her, so I only give her healthy food.

Kirby waits for her treats, but she has to eat all her rat food first.

Once in a while, we give Kirby a piece of hard-boiled egg or a piece of cheese. Plus Kirby gets a wheat flake every day as a special treat.

Wild rats eat grains, fruits, and vegetables just like Kirby does. That's why farmers think rats are pests. Wild rats also eat small animals such as frogs, lizards, birds, and fish. They'll eat any people's leftovers they can find. Rats are omnivorous, just like people. This means they'll eat both animals and plants.

People Food for Rats

For their basic diet, rats will eat prepared rat pellets or the homemade diet described on page 37. No matter which diet you choose, your rat will also need fruits and vegetables to be healthy. A full-grown rat needs about ⅛ to ¼ cup of fruits and vegetables each day.

When it comes to feeding a rat, the simplest rule is to give it a variety of foods.

Foods Rats Love

- cherries
- peaches
- grapes
- strawberries
- ripe bananas
- apples

- cheese
- crackers
- soup
- cereal
- yogurt
- hard-boiled eggs

- broccoli
- cooked green beans
- cooked sweet potatoes
- carrots
- peas
- tomatoes

Foods You Should Never Feed Your Rat*

- chocolate
- licorice
- raw beans
- raw sweet potatoes

- raw cabbage or brussels sprouts
- raw artichokes
- raw tofu

- green bananas
- green potato skins or eyes

Foods You Should Limit*

- corn
- beets
- celery

- eggplant
- lettuce
- cucumbers

- radishes
- spinach
- collards

*These foods contain substances called nitrates that may cause tumors in rats.

Sometimes I feed Kirby warm soup. I put it in her water bottle instead of water. She likes that. After she drinks all she wants, I clean the bottle and fill it up again with water.

I like to give Kirby a small dog biscuit, too. Rats like to have something to gnaw on. They also like wood blocks from pet stores. Like all rodents, rats have teeth that grow all their lives. By gnawing and also by grinding their teeth, they grind their teeth down. Otherwise, their teeth would get too long and they wouldn't be able to chew at all.

Drinking lots of liquids is important for rats, and so is gnawing. Kirby likes crunchy dog biscuits.

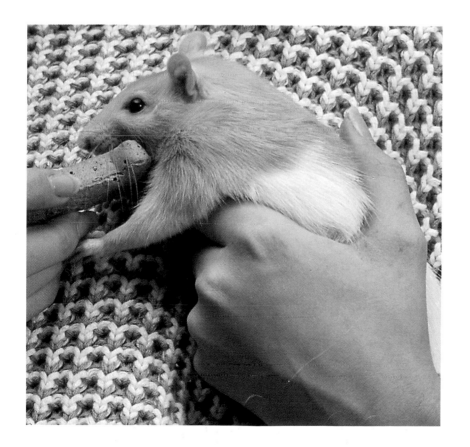

Pet rats are clean animals...

Some people think that Kirby is dirty, just because she's a rat. She's not dirty at all. Pet rats are very clean animals. They like a clean, dry cage. It's just up to you to keep it clean. You should clean a rat's cage a little bit every day. This is both for the rat and for you. A dirty cage can make a rat sick—especially with respiratory diseases. Plus, dirty cages smell.

Every day, either my dad or I check over Kirby's aquarium. First we scoop out her bathroom area with a litter scoop. We put the droppings into a plastic bag and throw that in the trash. Rats go to the bathroom in the same place each day, so this is easy.

Kirby doesn't need baths, because she washes herself.

I take out the food Kirby hides, so it doesn't spoil. We rinse her cage with bleach water to kill the germs.

We also have to poke around in Kirby's bedroom and look through the bedding for food. I always check the hay, too. Rats like to hide and save bits of food. I take out any fresh food I find hidden, so it won't spoil in Kirby's cage.

Every weekend, I do a big housecleaning of Kirby's aquarium. I scoop out all the bedding and throw it in the trash. I wash Kirby's hat and put it in the dryer. Then I fill a bucket with about 10 cups of warm water and 1 cup of bleach. I wet a small towel with the bleach water and wring it out. I wash the aquarium with the wet towel. I use an old knife to scrape any dirt from the aquarium's corners. Then I rinse the aquarium well.

Kirby likes to watch me
clean her cage.

While I'm cleaning Kirby's cage, Kirby needs to be someplace safe. I put her in a plastic bucket and keep her near me. Some people have found a bucket is a good place to keep a rat, when you can't keep an eye on it. It works pretty well with Kirby, though sometimes she climbs out.

Another thing I do with Kirby is let her roam around my room. I straighten up my room first. I don't want Kirby to make a mess of my things, or play with something that will hurt her.

I cover up the heat register, since I've heard rats will climb into them. A rat can even squeeze through the spaces between a window and an air conditioner. Rats will chew on anything, too. Once Kirby tried to chew on the Styrofoam around my air conditioner! I also put electrical cords out of reach, so Kirby won't chew on them. Most important, I make sure my bedroom door is shut. That way Kirby won't start walking all over the house.

We let Kirby run around the house sometimes, but we have to watch her. You can't be too careful with your rat, since rats will climb anywhere.

A Rat Likes

- Fresh food and water everyday
- A clean cage
- Exploring outside its cage
- Making nests and burrowing
- Playing with other rats
- Being around people
- Playing with you

A Rat Hates

- Stale food and dirty water
- A dirty cage
- Drafts
- Loud noises & bright lights
- Being too hot or too cold
- Not having somebody to play with everyday

Some rats like to swim.

As soon as they get out of the water, they like to be warm and dry.

I don't believe Kirby would hurt my hamsters. I keep them apart, just in case.

Kirby likes to explore my room. She likes to crawl around my bookshelf the best. Sometimes she checks out my hamsters. But I make sure they stay in their cage when Kirby's out. Rats and hamsters are natural enemies.

Kirby likes to be out of her cage, but she likes to go back to it, too. When I'm done washing Kirby's aquarium, I rub it with a thick towel to make sure it's dry. Sometimes I run my blow dryer over it. Rats like their cages to be dry. I put new bedding in the dry aquarium, and put back Kirby's bowls and water bottle. I hold and pet Kirby for a while, then put her into her nice clean house.

Kirby's the best rat ever...

Kirby is very smart. All rats are. Rats are the most intelligent of all rodent pets. Rats love to play games, and they can do lots of tricks. They learn quickly if you reward them with food. I decided to teach Kirby a few tricks when summer came. I stayed at my dad's house then, so I had more time to spend with Kirby, too.

The first trick I wanted Kirby to learn was her name, so she would come to me when I called her.

The first day I tried to teach Kirby her name, I set her on my bedroom floor. I sat just a few feet from her. I held up a cereal flake and said, "Kirby, come here."

The real trick is getting a rat to pay attention!

Of course Kirby came to me, because of the flake. But the next day I sat a little farther away from her. She was happy to come toward me again, because she knew that she was going to have a flake to eat.

Each day when I called Kirby, I moved a little farther away with the flake. Kirby usually came to me. Within a week, I could call Kirby and she would come from across the room.

After that first week, I didn't *always* give Kirby the flake. When Kirby came to me, I picked her up and cuddled her instead. In less than two weeks, Kirby came to me when I said "Kirby, come here."

Rats don't have good eyesight. But they hear well, and they'll respond to your voice.

Rats stand all the time. It's harder to get them to do it when you want them to.

The next trick I taught Kirby was how to stand on her hind legs. This was an easy trick. Rats like to stand on their hind legs. This position helps them explore their surroundings.

To get Kirby to stand up, I held a treat—like a corn flake or piece of strawberry—a few inches above her head. Then I said, "Stand." Kirby is smart. She wanted the treat, so she stood on her hind legs. I gave her the treat and said, "Good rat."

I tried this with Kirby for a few days. Soon Kirby knew what "stand" meant, so I started to do it without a treat in my hand. It was hiding in my pocket instead. I still gave her the treats after she stood. But after about a week, I didn't always give her a treat. Still, Kirby stood up when I put my hand over her head and said, "Stand." I always picked her up, cuddled her, and told her what a good rat she was.

I'm so impressed that Kirby is doing tricks because she likes me—not just for food. I think she's absolutely the best pet, just as good as a cat or a dog.

Kirby likes being cuddled, so it's as good as a treat.

By the time summer came, Kirby and I were really good friends. But I wondered if she could make friends with another rat. My friend Erica kept telling me it would be fun if Kirby met Alphonsia. We could have a rat race with them.

Erica didn't mean a race where Alphonsia and Kirby would be running around the room. Erica and I would each build a racing lane for our rat to race in. We'd put our rat in one end and a piece of salami or cheese at the other end. Then we'd see which rat would run the fastest to get the treat.

Rats are good runners, especially when they're running toward food.

When Erica came over to build our racetrack, she brought Alphonsia with her. I was glad that Alphonsia is another female. If Erica brought over a male rat that wasn't neutered, the rats could mate and Kirby could get pregnant. I've been thinking I'd like to get another rat. But if Kirby had babies, I'd have more rats than I want.

We built our racing lanes out of cardboard. Each rat needed a separate lane. Otherwise, they would get too interested in each other to race.

The rats watched us, but I don't think they knew what we had in mind.

Alphonsia won this race. Really the rats both won, since they both got treats.

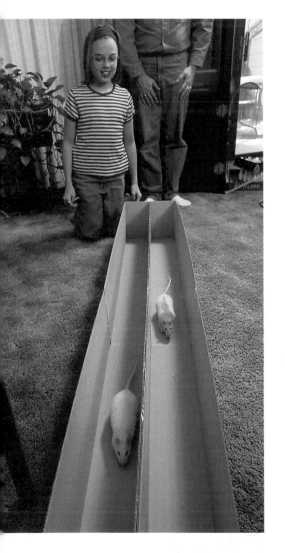

Before we started the race, Erica and I let our rats explore the new boxes. We also put food in the boxes, so our rats would know that getting into the racing lanes would be worth it.

When we finally started the race, Kirby scurried fast! Alphonsia moved along slowly, still exploring the box. When Kirby got to the end, I picked her up and cuddled her. "You are the best rat ever," I told her.

It took a few times for Alphonsia to realize that we wanted her to run a race, not explore.

The next day, we raced the rats again. Sometimes Alphonsia won. Sometimes Kirby did. Both rats seemed to be having fun and enjoying their snacks.

How to Make a Rat Racetrack

What you'll need:
- Long sheets of tagboard or cardboard
- Strong tape, such as packing tape
- Sharp scissors
- Ruler

What you'll do:

   To make one rat racing lane, cut the cardboard into 3 pieces as shown in the diagram below. If you don't have cardboard that's 5 feet long, you'll need to tape a few lengths of board together, before cutting. Then tape all the cardboard pieces together to form a long racing lane. Repeat these instructions to make a second lane. Then tape the two lanes together, side by side.

   Another way to make rat racing lanes is to tape together boxes from sandwich bags or kitchen wraps. The sides won't be as high, however, and the rats may become distracted.

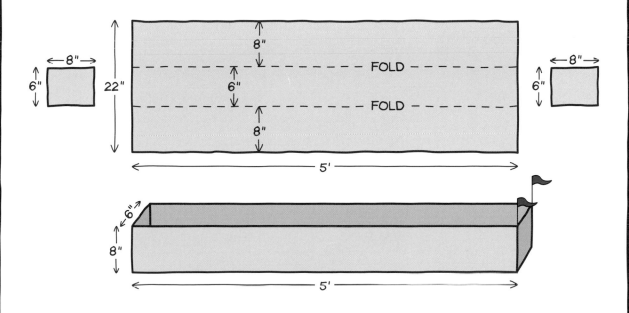

A few weeks later, I decided I'd like to build Kirby a maze. I saw one in a newsletter about rats. It was made from lots of boxes with holes in them. It's actually a rat playhouse, playground, and maze all in one.

To make the rat maze, I collected Kleenex boxes, milk cartons, different-sized little gift boxes, and those cardboard canisters from soft-drink mixes. Some boxes I painted with nontoxic paint. Other boxes I covered with colored paper. I cut doors in all the boxes so Kirby could walk from box to box. I connected the boxes with tape. Kirby loves exploring in it. My dad and I also made Kirby a Lego castle.

I like to make toys for Kirby. She needs new things to play with, so she doesn't get bored.

Sometimes I play with Kirby inside her cage.

Kirby loves to play "Fish," too. I made some tiny fish out of cardboard and attached them each to a string. I tied the other end of each string to a chopstick fishing pole. When I pull the fish along, Kirby tries to catch them. This game is also good rat exercise.

Kirby doesn't have a running wheel yet. I played with her so much during the summer, I think she's gotten enough exercise. But I'm going to buy her a running wheel, as a going-away present, when school starts and I go back to live with my mom. I hope it keeps Kirby from getting bored when I'm not there to play with her.

Who'll Get Along with Your Rat

Rats don't get along with hamsters, mice, or gerbils. They are natural enemies. Rats do get along well with other rats. Many people have more than one rat. Unless you want babies, make sure all your rats are the same sex, or have them neutered or spayed by a veterinarian.

If you start with one rat and bring in a new one, put the newcomer into a separate cage. Otherwise, the two rats will fight. Then introduce your rats to each other gradually, for about 20 minutes a day. Make the introductions in a neutral place—such as the bathtub—not one cage or the other. It could take a few weeks for the rats to become friends.

If you have pets like lizards or fish, keep them in a room that's separate from your rat, and in a covered aquarium. Rats like to eat fresh fish. Your rat might also attack a small lizard.

Dogs, cats, and rats have been known to become friends. But make sure that the friendship is well supervised. This means *keep your eyes on them at all times*. If your rat seems scared, or if your cat or dog seems to want to pounce, don't push the relationship. Most often, friendships between rats and canines or felines develop if the dog or cat is a puppy or kitten when it meets the rat.

Kirby is a good pet and a good friend.

I'll miss being with Kirby every day, but my dad promises to take good care of her when I'm not here. I know he will, since he's had a lot of practice already. I've also taught him a lot about rats.

Rats are playful, interesting, and fun. I'm sure glad my dad bought me Kirby, and that we've gotten to know each other so well. She's an entertaining and lovable pet.

Glossary

Burrow: to dig and live in holes and tunnels. Wild rats burrow in the ground.

Diarrhea (dye-uh-*ree*-uh): a condition in which an animal has runny stools (poops). Diarrhea is a sign of an unhealthy diet or an illness.

Neuter (*noo*-ter): to remove the sex organs (testicles) from a male animal so that it is unable to reproduce

Nocturnal (nok-*ter*-nuhl): active mainly at night

Nutrients (*noo*-tree-uhnts): the different substances in food that are needed by people, animals, and plants for good health. Examples of nutrients are proteins, minerals, and vitamins.

Omnivorous (ahm-*nih*-vuh-russ): feeding on both plants and animals

Respiratory (*ress*-pi-ruh-tor-ee): having to do with the breathing process—involving the nose, throat, and lungs. Signs of respiratory infection or disease are sniffling, sneezing, or a runny nose or eyes.

Rodent (*rho*-dunt): a small animal with large, sharp teeth that it uses for gnawing

Spay: to remove the sex organs (uterus and ovaries) from a female animal so that it is unable to reproduce

Weaned: having started to eat and drink foods other than mother's milk

Resources

Rat Fan Club
Debbie Ducommun
857 Lindo Lane
Chico, CA 95926
(916) 899-0605
e-mail: ratlady@sunset.net

Rat, Mouse, & Hamster Fanciers
Membership: Sylvia Butler
188 School Street
Danville, CA 94526
(510) 820-9171
http://www.geocities.com/Heartland/Prairie/2009

Rat & Mouse Club of America
Mary Ann Isaksen
13075 Springdale Street, Suite 302
Westminster, CA 92683
(714) 892-7523
e-mail: RMCA1@aol.com
http://www.rmca.org

Northeast Rat & Mouse Club
Membership: Pat Smouse
1775 Smouse Lane SE
Flintstone, MD 21530
(301) 777-8234
e-mail: patriciasmouse@netbiz.net
http://www.bucknell.edu/~dmiddltn/nrmci.html

For Further Reading

Bailey, Jill. *Discovering Rats and Mice.* New York: Bookwright Press, 1987.

Fischer-Nagel, Heiderose and Andreas. *A Look through the Mouse Hole.* Minneapolis: Carolrhoda, 1989.

Fox, Susan. *Rats.* Neptune City, NJ: T.F.H. Publications, 1983.

Glaser, Linda. *Rosie's Birthday Rat.* Illustrated by Nancy Poydar. New York: Delacorte Press, 1996 (fiction).

Henrie, Fiona. *Mice and Rats.* New York: Franklin Watts, 1980.

Kouts, Anne. *Kenny's Rat.* Illustrated by Betty Fraser. New York: Viking Press, 1970 (fiction).

Levitin, Sonia. *Rita, the Weekend Rat.* Illustrated by Leonard Shortall. New York: Atheneum, 1971 (fiction).

Pope, Joyce. *Taking Care of Your Mice and Rats.* New York: Franklin Watts, 1987.

Powell, E. Sandy. *Rats.* (Early Bird Nature Series.) Photographs by Jerry Boucher. Minneapolis: Lerner, 1994.

Sproule, Anna. *Mice and Rats.* New York: Bookwright Press, 1989.

Index

ABOUT THE AUTHOR
Arlene Erlbach has written more than 30 books of fiction and nonfiction for young people. In addition to being an author, Ms. Erlbach is an elementary school teacher. She loves to encourage children to read and write, and she is in charge of her school's Young Authors program. Ms. Erlbach lives in Morton Grove, Illinois, with her husband, her son, a collie, and two cats. She was born in the year of the rat.

ABOUT THE PHOTOGRAPHER
Andy King is a native of Boulder, Colorado, and a graduate of Colorado State University. He has traveled around the world as a documentary and corporate photographer, and he has worked as a photographer at newspapers in Minnesota and Texas. He lives with his wife, Patricia, and their daughter in St. Paul, Minnesota, where he enjoys mountain biking and playing basketball.